@thetable

JOHN CALDWELL

ISBN: 9798320171104

DEDICATION

This research project is dedicated to anyone who has ever found themselves stuck in the closet, not knowing how to get out. Your experience is valid and very real for a lot of people. This project shines a light on those experiences and hopes to foster empathy and inclusivity among families with children and young adults who identify with the LGBTQIA+ community.

Introduction

"I'm Gay." Two words heard by parents at dinner tables across the nation. What happens in the moments after this statement are crucial for the relationship between parents and LGBTQIA+ adolescents. Positive reactions can lead to healthy, flourishing relationships and reduce risk factors that are so often associated with the LGBTQIA+ community. Negative reactions, however, can cause emotional and even physical harm to the wellbeing of a lesbian, gay, bisexual, transgender, questioning, intersex, or asexual adolescent. In this exploration of issues surrounding the LGBTQIA+

community, I plan to equip you with the tools you need to, at most, support and encourage your LGBTQIA+ adolescent, and at least, help you in becoming a needed ally. Through scholarly research and personal accounts, I hope to offer a detailed perspective of the atrocities LGBTQIA+ youth experience and how we can work together to change the mindsets and biases that cause them.

The Problem

As a gay man myself, I have experienced many of the same things I will talk about in my research. My father discovered I was gay when I was roughly 13 years old. I was in my room, privately looking at pictures of shirtless men on an iPod touch I had saved up to buy. My father barged in without knocking, as he often did, making me jump and quickly lock my iPod. He then forced me to unlock it, revealing pictures of attractive shirtless men. With a shocked look of disgust, my father ran downstairs to talk with my stepmom. What felt like an eternity passed as I had a panic attack in my on-suite bathroom. I started hyperventilating and after a few minutes was able to bring myself together before my father called for me to come down and talk with them. An intense few-hour interrogation followed before my father made me watch as he took a hammer to the iPod Touch I had bought. After smashing it to bits, he put the pieces in a zip-lock bag and hung it over the kitchen sink to remind me every day how much they hated me.

This was the beginning of continuous abuse I endured from my father and stepmother. They used everything they could to punish me. Taking game systems away, selling my alto-saxophone, even taking books that I enjoyed reading away so that my existence was limited to the basic things one needs to survive: food, water, sleep, and shelter, not to mention an endless list of chores I had to complete each day. They made me into a shell of a human, not allowing me to even enjoy family movie nights together. Instead, I would have to scrub the kitchen floor with a rag while they watched "The Avengers".

While my experience may seem extreme, I'm not alone. In a study conducted by The Journal of the American Medical Association, many high school students experience discrimination, stigma, and bullying in the adolescent years both at school and at home. These experiences can lead to students feeling worthless, having thoughts of suicide, and some even deciding to take their own life. In this study that took a broad sample of high schools across the United States, out of 9-12 grade LGB and questioning students, a staggering 549,980 of them have seriously considered suicide, 490,870 have made a suicide plan, and 120,790 students had a suicide attempt that resulted in an injury that required medical attention. It's clear that we have a glaring problem that needs urgent attention, discussion, and immediate actions taken to protect LGBTQIA+ adolescents.

549,980 students considered suicide

490,870 students made suicide plan

120,790

had attempt that resulted in serious injury.

Origins

Where do these conversations of discrimination toward the LGBTQIA+ community originate? Well, most of us have experienced it from the earliest stages of adolescence. As we are developing into adults in these early, emerging stages, we tend to experience a deep desire to be "normal". We want to be cool and fit in, and anything outside of that paradigm plunges us into social ruin that has the potential to shake our emotional, mental, and even physical lives.

In a study conducted by a university in the Midwest, several doctoral candidates of social work embarked on a journey to discover the impact the phrase, "That's so gay!" could have on the physical, emotional, and mental wellbeing of college students. The results concluded that the use of the phrase from heterosexual people among those apart of the LGB community had direct, negative correlations to specific health factors including their feeling of acceptance, self-esteem, anxiety, headaches, trouble eating, and comfort talking about their sexual orientation. Using this phrase in a negative, mocking manner, aligning being gay to an undesirable action or way of being truly has an impact on those of us in the LGBTQIA+ community.

Another source of negative thoughts and stereotypes surrounding those in the LGBTQIA+ community come from religious points of view. When conducting my research, a local educator reached out to offer a bit of perspective on this topic. "A large part of our community considers themselves Christian, and, as such, they use that as an excuse to hurl bigoted statements." (Respondent #3) Her sentiments give light to the profoundly tragic impact religion can have on perpetuating untrue and unfair accusations and opinions of the LGBTQIA+ community, giving a footing to the hatred so many have toward us. Religion can have a quite manipulative and persuasive way of getting people to think and act a certain way, making it difficult to reason and share empathy with those that are different than them. This rigidity can, in the most extreme cases, lend to hate crimes and tragic violence where those committing these acts feel "compelled by God" to do so.

> *"A large part of our community considers themselves Christian, and, as such, they use that as an excuse to hurl bigoted statements."*

What You Can Do

At the beginning of this research project, I posted on Facebook asking for input from parents, educators, allies, and others. While my initial post only garnered one response, after urging more to respond through posting it again with an emphatic plea for help, I received a few eye-opening responses. One local parent responded," As far as talking to my kid about LGBTQIA+, I'm not sure that she has the mental competence to understand it." (Respondent #2) When asked a follow-up question about what that conversation might look like when her child gets older and may be able to understand it a bit more, she responded: "I'm not entirely sure. Let me think about it and I'll get back to you." (Respondent #2) This knee-jerk reaction is not uncommon among parents both that are raising heterosexual children and parents that have an adolescent who has come out to them. Even in my own research, it was difficult to find solid scholarly research in this area, perhaps because many are so afraid of it.

In a study published in The Family Journal entitled Family Support Would Have Been Like Amazing: LGBTQ Youth Experiences with Parental and Family Support, Stuart Roe conducted ground-breaking research on what LGBTQIA+ youth experience within their homes and what support, or lack thereof looks like for adolescents who come out as part of the LGBTQIA+ community. From his research emerged four things you should know about what LGBTQIA+ youth experience.

1

COMING OUT IS NECESSARY

The first of these is that coming out is necessary. In a response from one of the students interviewed for the study, the necessity of coming out is revealed as a step in preserving his mental health. "Yeah, I had to, it was like really, really, really, really messing me up just hiding it every single day or putting effort into hiding it…it felt much better just to be myself." (Marco 57) His sentiments illustrate the immense pressure placed on those apart of the LGBTQIA+ community that have yet to come out of the closet and are still struggling to accept who they are. As a gay man myself, I've experienced this pervasive feeling that siphons your energy, physical and mental strength, and can even make you do extreme things to prove to others that you are not indeed gay. I remember in middle school, buying flowers, cards, and gifts for the most popular girls in school, simply because I wanted to prove to everyone that I wasn't gay.

2

PARENT RESPONSE IS OFTEN NOT POSITIVE

The second thing Roe found during this study is that the initial response from parents is most often not a positive one. One tragic experience shared by Jonathan in his interview illustrates the sometimes-extreme rejection experienced by LGBTQIA+ youth. During a conversation talking about how his parents took him to court after coming out, Jonathan says "They wrote a letter disowning me and signing it at the bottom saying for homosexuality [and a host of other behaviors]." (Roe 57) I honestly teared up when I first read that during my research. While I did not go as far as a courtroom when being disowned by my family, I did experience some of the same forms of hatred and rejection of my identity by family and friends. I can't imagine having that played out in front of strangers in a courtroom. These knee-jerk responses must stop and be replaced by more supportive, positive actions taken by parents, family, and friends.

3

RELIGION AS A BARRIER TO SUPPORT

As discussed briefly in an earlier section, Roe also found that LGBTQ youth view religion as a barrier to support from parents. During his research, he found that "Many of the students interviewed were previously involved in the churches attended by their parents, but as they became more aware of their sexuality, they decided not to attend." (Roe 57) One respondent detailed his experience when talking privately with leadership of the church he attended. Devin, one of the students interviewed during the study, remembers his experience of dealing with church leadership regarding his sexuality. "Yeah, like what did they call it, you need to recant your ways or pray or something to fix it, and I was like, it is not something to be fixed and it is me, and eventually the church said, well if you are not going to even try to fix yourself then why come? And since then, I haven't gone." (Devin 57) Devin went on to say, "I don't go to church anymore because, I don't think, I don't think I'd be accepted at the church I used to go, so I don't..., I don't know." (Devin 57) Devin's experience is not uncommon. I, myself, grew up in a Christian household that took religion quite seriously. I was even part of leadership in my youth group as a worship leader, on the worship team, and volunteered during the summer at my church. After going off to a Christian college, I realized that my religion and sexuality were incompatible. I eventually left all of it behind in search of what being a good human could look like outside of the confines of bigoted religious circles.

4

YOUTH WANT EXPLICIT SUPPORT FROM PARENTS

The fourth and final finding of Roe's study was that youth want explicit support and encouragement from their parents, family, and friends. He explains, "Improving relationships between LGBTQ youth and their parents is important for the health and well-being of LGBTQ youth, but very little is known about how to improve that relationship." (Roe 58). Throughout this research I've found that the most important thing in this area is to avoid the knee-jerk reaction that so often occurs within family settings and offer an individualistic approach, urging the adolescent to pursue who they want to be, similar to the age-old adage of "Chase Your Dreams!". All we really want is support and empathy from our family and providing even the slightest affirmation of who we are can have profound implications for the success and well-being of your emerging adult.

"Yeah, like what did they call it, you need to recant your ways or pray or something to fix it, and I was like, it is not something to be fixed and it is me, and eventually the church said, well if you are not going to even try to fix yourself then why come? And since then, I haven't gone."

Receiving love, acceptance, empathy, and encouragement from others outside of the LGBTQIA+ can be quite challenging, if it happens at all. Perhaps this phenomenon is due to the lack of education on the topic. Stereotypes fly around us every day, whether it's in church settings, social media, or even family dinner table discussions, these unfair stereotypes of the LGBTQIA+ community are often skewed and disappointing. Marvin Hoffman, a high school English teacher, recognized this in a research project he conducted with a group of students in a creative writing class. He embarked on a courageous journey of teaching LGBTQIA+ literature in the classroom. Students were given the option to participate or not, keeping a journal the entire time of their thoughts and reflections of the impact the literature had on them. The work in question was a play entitled, "Torch Song", a gay love story between two male characters. One of the students involved in the study reflects:

"This play was really the one that made homosexuality seem not like just a bunch of sex, but of feelings and pain. I think it was the only one that dealt with the social problems of homosexuality, which is something I think has to be mentioned. Arnold summed it up for us when he says to his mother" ... try to imagine the world the other way around. Imagine that every movie, book, magazine, TV show, newspaper, commercial, billboard, told you that you should be homosexual. But you know that you're not and you know that for you this is right...." That scenario made me think about it and for the first time I began to really understand how awkward it would be."

This quote reflects a level of empathy that can grow, even among high school students, toward the LGBTQIA+ community and help them to better understand what we experience and the impact their understanding has the potential to have. The same respondent went on to say:

"I see now that their relationships are very similar to ours. They feel everything that we do, maybe even more in some cases, like here, since Ed is bisexual. I feel it is bad how people discriminate against gays, because it's their private life and they can do what and how they feel. I wonder how this world would be if being gay would be normal and heterosexuality would be viewed as a sin. By reading this book I was exposed to a homosexual, and I realized that they are people too. They think, feel, and love." (Hoffman)

The experience described by this student during a study of LGBTQIA+ literature is perhaps the cornerstone of the empathy and support LGBTQIA+ individuals so desperately crave from their parents, family, friends, and society. By seeing gay, lesbian, bisexual, transgender, questioning, intersex, and asexual individuals as real people with feelings and emotions, dreams, and aspirations, maybe we could work together to form a more mutual understanding of each other. We do, after all, "think, feel, and love." (Hoffman).

Perhaps the most important take-away from my research is that LGBTQIA+ people need support from the earliest stages of accepting who they are. You have an incredible opportunity to step in and be that support they need at a critical time in their journey toward adulthood. This support can take many shapes and forms and may not even need to address their sexuality directly. When I was discovering this about myself in my developing stages of middle and high school, having supportive teachers, librarians, choir directors, coaches, and others helped me become more confident in who I am as a whole person including my sexuality. While it took me a bit more time to be completely solid in my identity as a gay man, I still remember the impacts, both positive and negative, others had on my experience, even without their explicit support of my sexuality. Most did not know that I was gay but were encouraging and supportive regardless. You now have at your disposal, a few powerful tools to make an enormous impact on someone you know who is part of the LGBTQIA+ community, or might be closeted, hoping to find someone just like you to support and encourage them in their journey.

Resources

1) Hoffman, Marvin. "Teaching "Torch Song": Gay Literature in the Classroom." English Journal, vol. 82, no. 5, 1993, pp. 55-58.

2) Moita-Lopes, Luiz P. "Queering Literacy Teaching: Analyzing Gay-Themed Discourses in a Fifth-Grade Class in Brazil." Journal of Language, Identity, and Education, vol. 5, no. 1, 2006, pp. 31-50.

3) Respondent #1 - Local Parent

4) Respondent #2 - Local Parent

5) Respondent #3 - Local Educator

6) Respondent #4 - Local Educator and member of LGBTQIA+ community

*Identities of local respondents have been kept anonymous as to protect them from potential discrimination and retaliation from employers, family, friends, and others who might take discriminatory action against them. *

7) Roe, Stuart. "Family Support would have been Like Amazing: LGBTQ Youth Experiences with Parental and Family Support." The Family Journal (Alexandria, Va.), vol. 25, no. 1, 2017, pp. 55-62.

8) Woodford, Michael R., et al. ""that's

so Gay!": Examining the Covariates of Hearing this Expression among Gay, Lesbian, and Bisexual College Students." Journal of American College Health, vol. 60, no. 6, 2012, pp. 429-434.

9) Zaza, Stephanie, Laura Kann, and Lisa C. Barrios. "Lesbian, Gay, and Bisexual Adolescents: Population Estimate and Prevalence of Health Behaviors." JAMA : The Journal of the American Medical Association, vol. 316, no. 22, 2016, pp. 2355-2356.

ABOUT THE AUTHOR

John Caldwell is a college student, musician, entrepreneur, and LGBTQIA+ rights activist living in Jonesboro, Arkansas. He is passionate about making the world a better, more inclusive place by sharing his story and bringing light to real issues that plague our community.

www.ingramcontent.com/pod-product-compliance
Lightning Source LLC
Chambersburg PA
CBHW051411250726
48656CB00010B/2270
9798320171104